ZIGGY'S FOLLIES

Other Ziggy Books

Ziggy in the Fast Lane
Ziggy's Ups and Downs
Ziggy's Place
Alphabet Soup Isn't Supposed to Make Sense
Ziggy's Big Little Book

ZIGGY'S FOLLIES ®

by Tom Wilson

Andrews and McMeel
A Universal Press Syndicate Company
Kansas City • New York

ATTENTION: SCHOOLS AND BUSINESSES

Andrews and McMeel books are available at quantity discounts with bulk purchase for educational, business, or sales promotional use. For information, please write to: Special Sales Department, Andrews and McMeel, 4900 Main Street, Kansas City, Missouri 64112.

ALUMINUM CHRISTMAS TREES $39.95
...I'M GLAD JOYCE KILMER DIDN'T LIVE TO SEE THIS...
TOM WILSON

WATCHES AND CLOCKS
THERE'S NO PRESENT LIKE THE TIME!
TOM WILSON

9

11

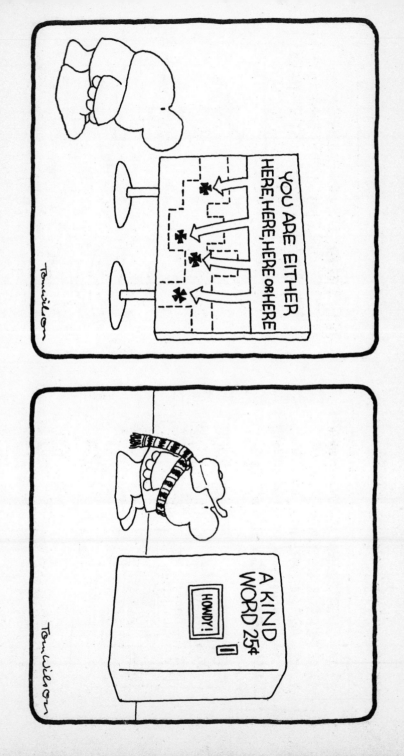

14

16

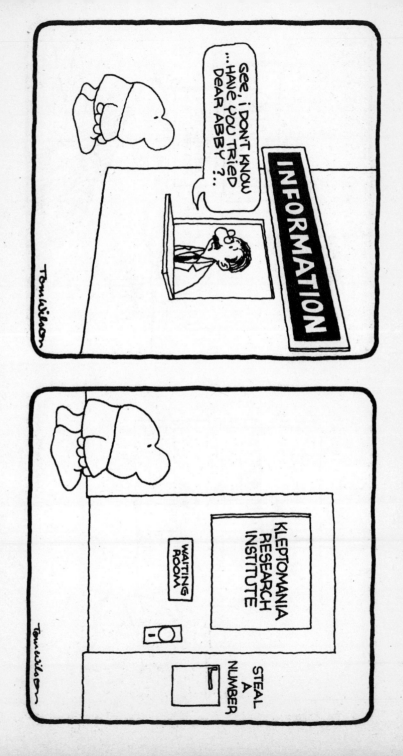

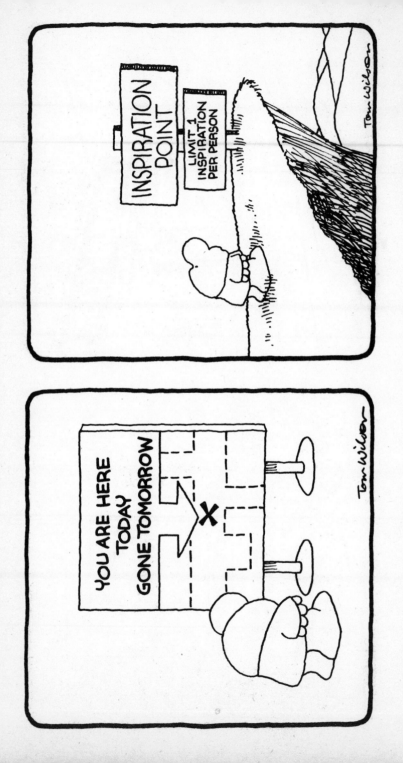

... IT'LL BE A WHILE ON YOUR TRANSACTION! .. WHILE YOU'RE WAITING, HOW 'BOUT A GAME OF DONKEY KONG?
BANK MONEY MACHINE
INSERT CARD HERE
Tom Wilson

YOU ARE HERE
THE PITS
Tom Wilson

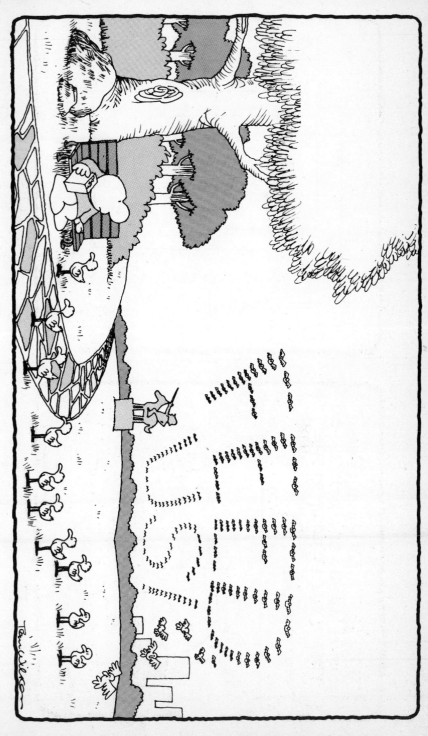

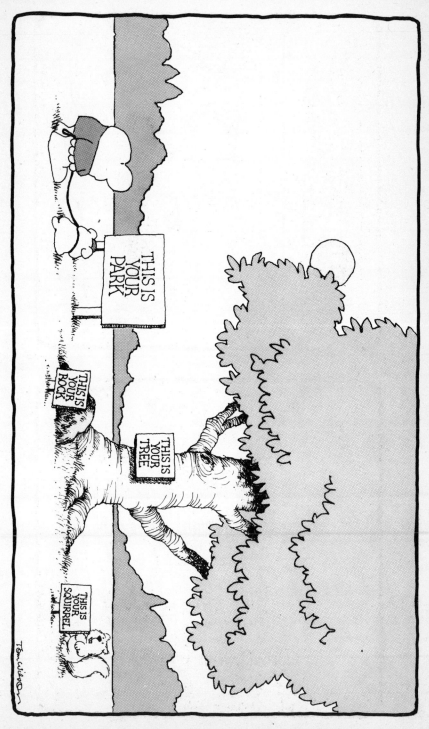

38

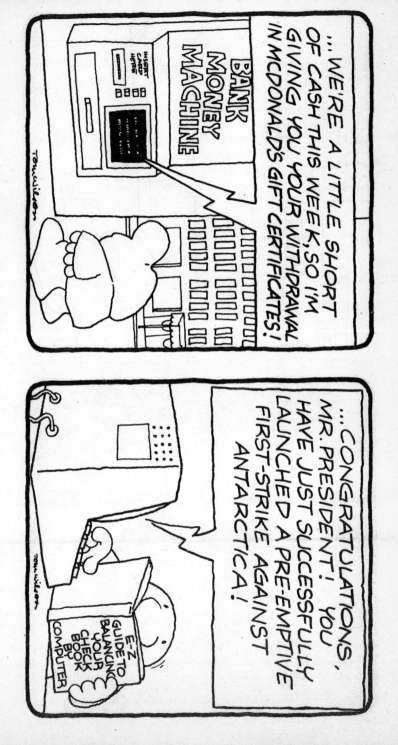

41

The Seven Warning Signs of Breakfast

I'M NOT AFRAID OF THE DARK ...ITS THE STUFF IN THE DARK THAT I'M SCARED OF!

47

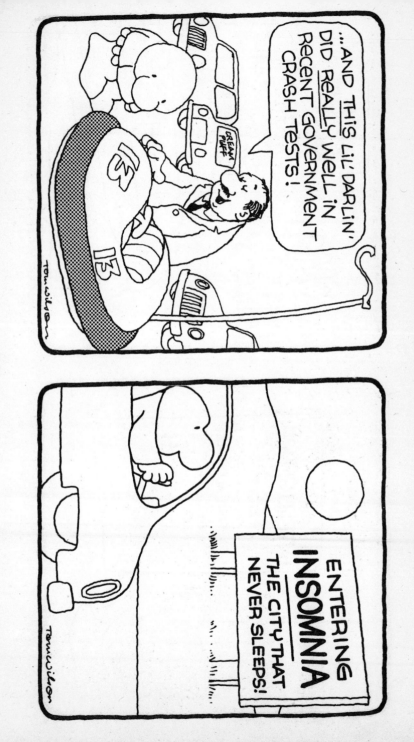

50

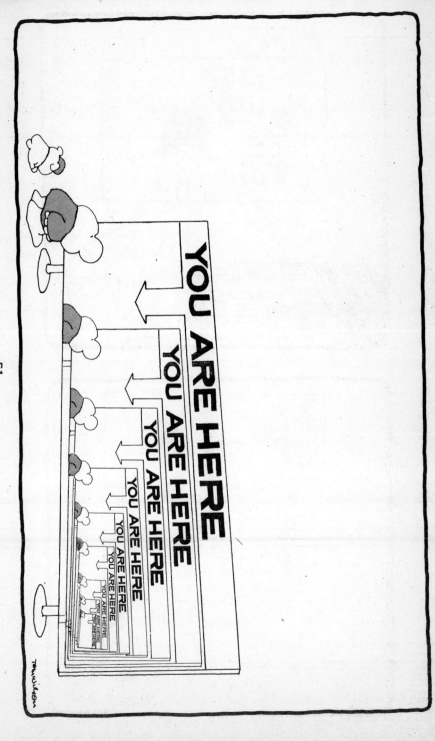

53

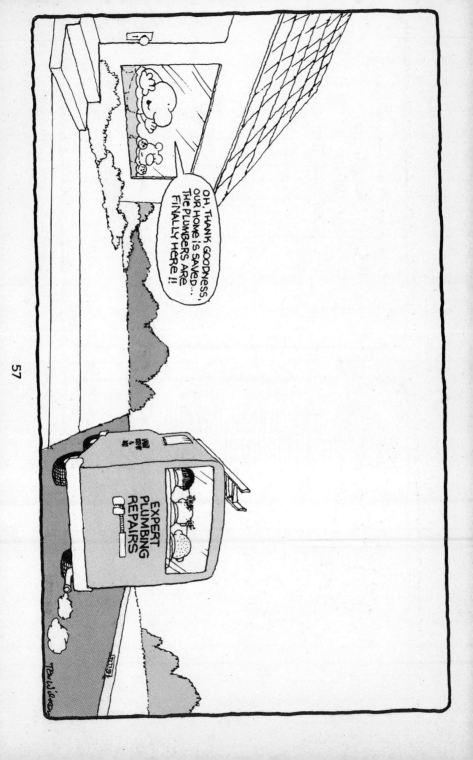

57

IN
OUT
THAT GRAY AREA IN BETWEEN
TOM WILSON

OOPS...SORRY, SIR, TELL YOU WHAT... THAT SOUP'S ON THE HOUSE!
TOM WILSON

MIGHTY FUNNY WEATHER LATELY!
Tom Wilson

...YOU KNOW YOUR LIFE IS TOO MUNDANE WHEN YOUR CLOSEST BRUSH WITH GREATNESS IS A LETTER FROM ED MCMAHON!
YOU MAY ALREADY BE A WINNER!
ED MCMAHON
ZIGGY
Tom Wilson

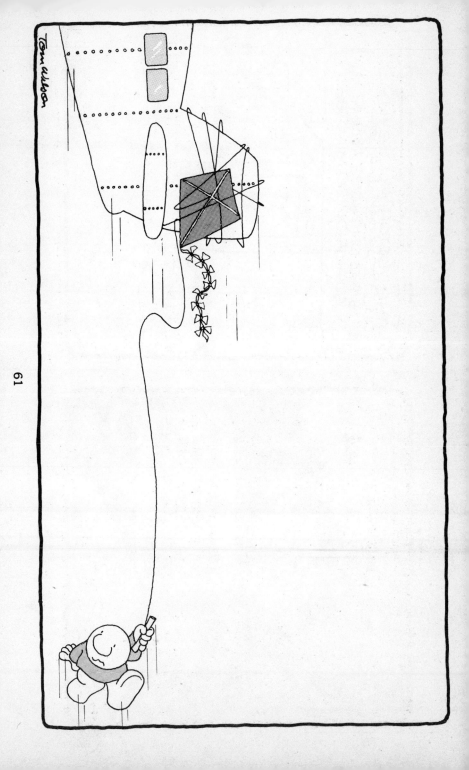

64

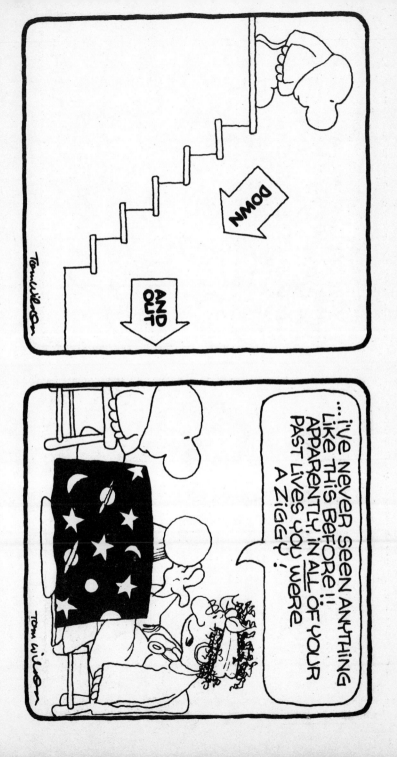

...YOU CAUGHT ME AT A BAD TIME ... OUR STOCKS ARE PRETTY LOW RIGHT NOW...THE ONLY WISHES I COULD POSSIBLY GRANT YOU ARE A DREAM DATE WITH DON RICKLES OR AN UNBREAKABLE PLASTIC POCKET COMB.

...THIS IS POSITIVELY THE WORST CASE OF ANIMAL MAGNETISM I'VE EVER SEEN!

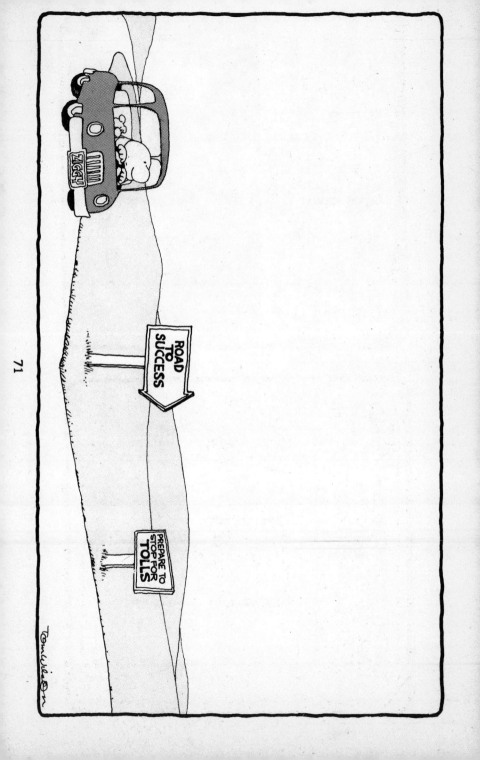

72

INSPIRATION POINT
PATENT APPLICATIONS
Tom Wilson

CLEM'S LAST CHANCE DINER
FRESH CATCH OF THE DAY
Rattlesnake
Tom Wilson

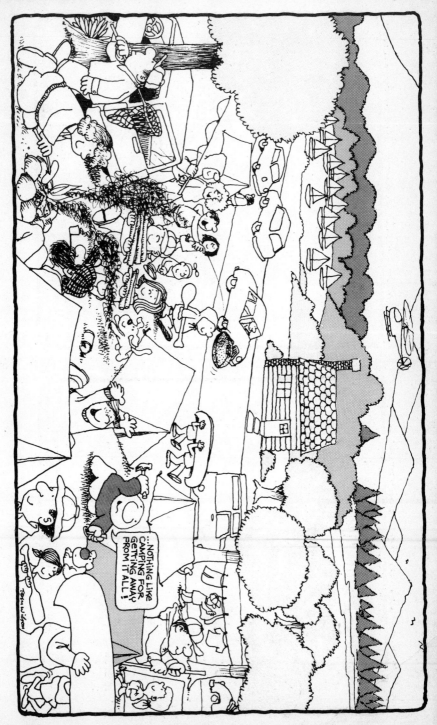

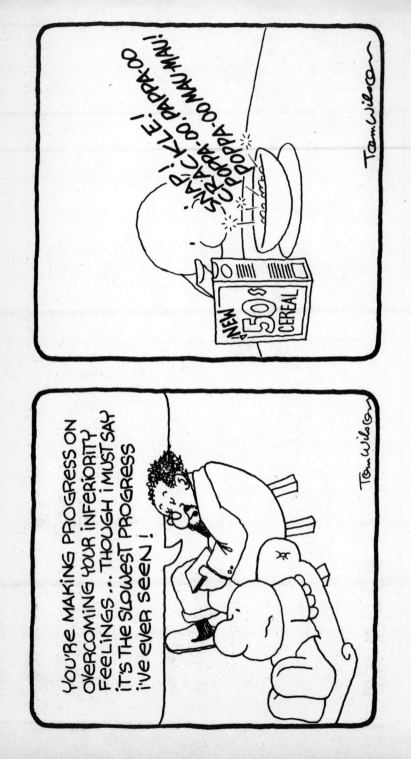

84

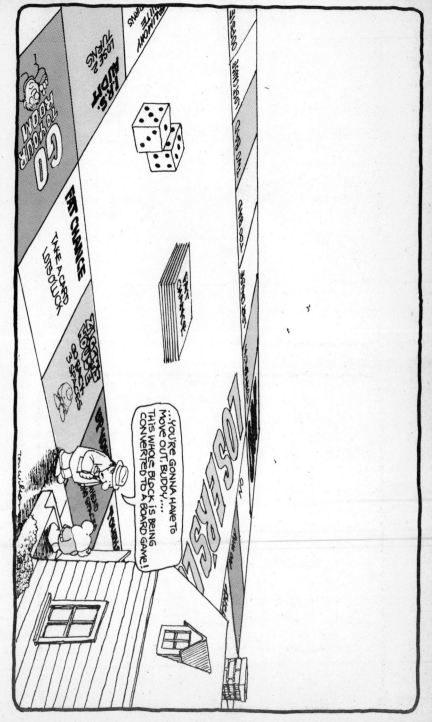

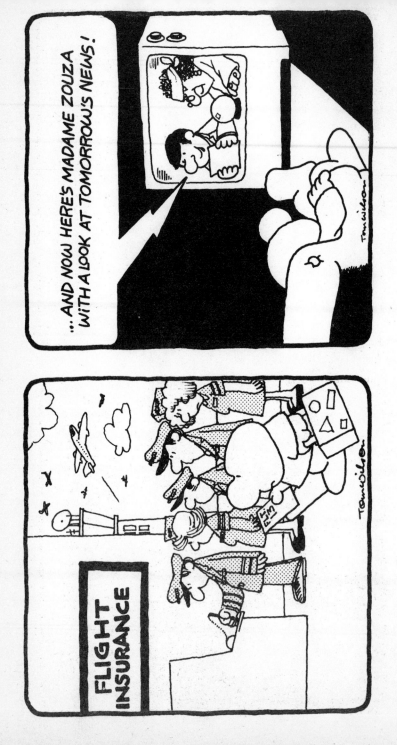

IT'S _NOT_ A BIRTH DEFECT...
A LOT OF CARTOON CHARACTERS
ARE DRAWN WITHOUT EARS !!

TONIGHT'S WEATHER WILL
BE PROBABLE, FOLLOWED
BY A PARTLY IFFY TOMORROW...

90

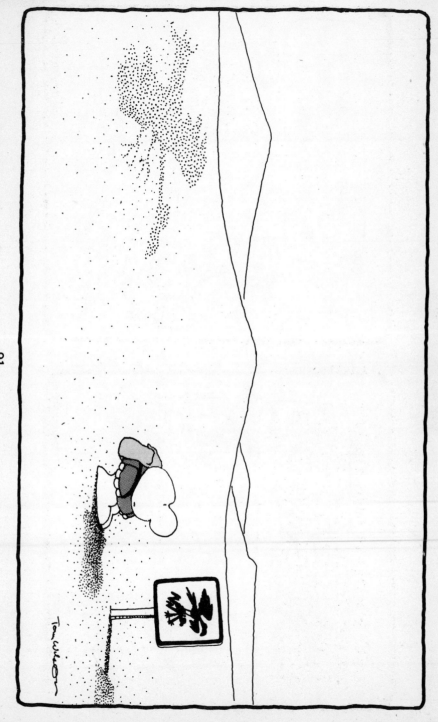

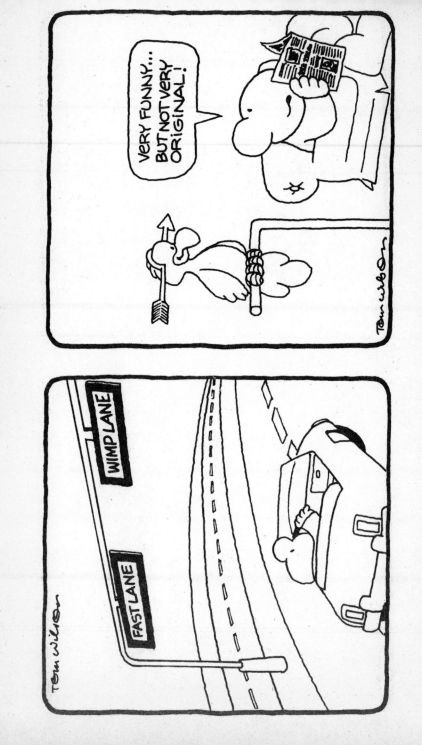

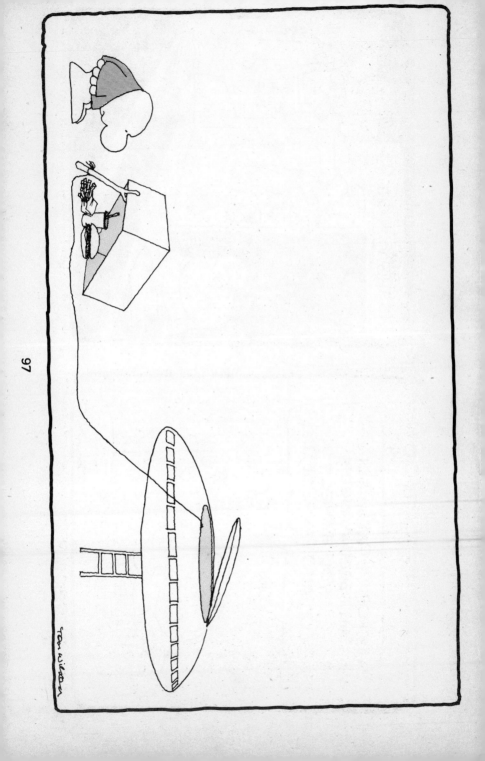

...FOR 79¢ WORTH OF BIRD SEED A WEEK ....YOU EXPECT LUCIANO PAVAROTTI?!
TOM WILSON

...IS THIS YOUR CAT?!
HAMAYOSHI'S SUSHI BAR
TOM WILSON

102

103

FUNG'S
CHINESE
RESTAURANT
SPECIAL
ALL YOU
CAN EAT
$2.00
...THEY ONLY GIVE YOU 1 CHOPSTICK!
TOM WILSON

HEY, NO PROBLEM!...
...HEY, NO PROBLEM!...
...HEY, NO PROBLEM!...
TOM WILSON